This book celebrates the arrival of

my dog's first year

a journal

POP PRESS

in case of loss, please return to:

contents

life is better with a dog

Welcome to your journal for your new dog's first year with you. Whether you have just welcomed a puppy into your home or adopted an older dog, this is the place where you can record all of the magical memories you'll share together over the next year. This book will also provide you with information on how to prepare for their arrival, as well as handy tips for training, and fun activities that you and your pup can do together to build trust.

Every dog is different and has a unique personality and set of characteristics. It can sometimes take a while to learn about their likes and dislikes or how to tell what mood they're in based on their behaviour. You can use the notes sections as a place to document your new buddy's development over the next year, as well as writing down things you learn about them along the way, or even any funny or sweet moments you want to remember.

Getting a dog of any age takes a lot of hard work (and energy!), but it is also a very exciting and rewarding time. We hope that this journal will be helpful and that it will also be something you can look back through to remember the special moments you will experience together over the next year.

stick your dog's
photo here

about my dog

born on

....

weighed

....

colour

....

markings

....

he/she had .... siblings

we first heard about our dog from

....

....

we chose this breed because

....

....

....

....

we first visited our new dog on

....

our dog's name

....

this was chosen because

....

....

....

our dog's mum is called

....

her story

....

....

our dog's dad is called

his story

_____

_____

_____

_____

_____

_____

_____

_____

_____

_____

_____

_____

_____

_____

NOTES

dog-proofing our home

To get ready for our dog's arrival, we:

- Put away treasured possessions they might chew, swallow or knock over.

- Added a baby gate for rooms they aren't allowed in.

- Removed poisonous plants – such as lilies.

- Tidied away electrical wires, small children's toys, etc.

- Made the garden fences secure – no holes!

For our dog's arrival we bought:

- Water bowl
- Food bowl
- Bed
- Crate
- Puppy pads
- Collar
- ID tags
- Lead
- Harness
- Grooming brush
- Stain remover!
- Toys
- Food
- Treats

ruff stuff

did you know?

Contrary to popular belief, dogs do not sweat by salivating. They sweat through the pads of their feet.

home is where
the dog is

our dog came home on

....

about the journey

....

....

....

....

....

Photos of our dog's first day with us!

tips for
the first days
at home

At home

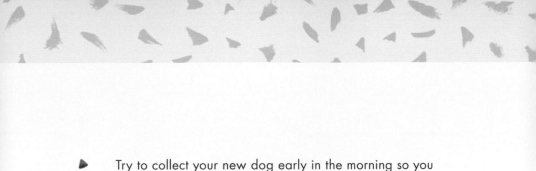

- Try to collect your new dog early in the morning so you have the rest of the day to settle them in.

- As soon as you arrive home, take them outside to have a wee.

- Once back inside, offer your dog some water and maybe a little food.

- Set an alarm for every half an hour and take your dog back outside for another wee. Be prepared for accidents!

- Let your dog explore their new surroundings but with constant supervision.

- Slowly introduce other people and animals.

- Make sure children know not to be rough – no pulling of ears, whiskers or tail.

- If your dog is a puppy, carry them up steps (and discourage jumping for their first year).

- If using a crate, make it comfy, and keep the door open so that they can go in and out. Perhaps leave a few pieces of food in there to show it is a happy place.

the first things our dog did in our home

....

....

....

....

....

things that went really well

....

....

....

things we need to work on

....

....

....

NOTES

hush puppy

our dog's bed is in

....

....

we made it cosy by

....

....

we helped them sleep by

....

....

....

things we need to work on

did you know?

Your dog needs plenty of opportunities to rest and for peace and quiet in the first few days, so make sure they have a comfy bed to go to.

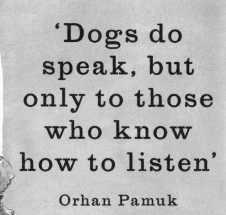

'Dogs do
speak, but
only to those
who know
how to listen'

Orhan Pamuk

paws for pawsterity

Here are our dog's paw prints

Date ....

'The journey
of life is
sweeter
when
travelled
with a dog'

doggy food diary

There are lots of things to consider when it comes to feeding routines as each dog is different.

- Most adult dogs should eat twice a day (puppies three times a day), once in the morning and once in the evening, but always check with your vet.

- Feed your dog in the same place each day – this will help establish a routine and make them feel safe.

- Do not leave food lying around (throw any uneaten food away after 20 minutes): teaching them to eat straightaway will help their metabolism and will also help you to recognise if they're ill based on a lack of appetite.

- You can use mealtimes as an opportunity to reinforce training by making them sit and wait for your command before they eat.

Dogs thrive on routine when it comes to food and do not need variety. Use the table below to help you keep a record of what works best so that you can establish a routine as soon as possible and adjust food intake as necessary.

DAY	TIMES OF DAY	WHAT KIND OF FOOD	TREATS
sunday			
monday			
tuesday			
wednesday			
thursday			
friday			
saturday			

things that worked well

....

....

....

things we will try in the future

....

....

....

our dog's eating spot

....

....

favourite meal

....

....

first time our dog ate a new food

....

first time they ate fruit or vegetables

....

our dog's favourite treat

....

....

'The better
I get to know
men, the more
I find myself
loving dogs'

Charles de Gaulle

tips for
training

- Training should be fun and for the dog it should feel like play.

- Stay calm and relaxed – your dog can sense your feelings.

- Use praise when they have done well – say 'Good', stroke or pat them, or use a toy or treats.

- It is hard to understand humans, so don't tell your dog off when they don't understand. Also, don't reward bad behaviour with any extra attention. Instead, be clearer about what you do want your dog to do and reinforce their good behaviour.

- Keep training sessions short – 10–15 minutes two to three times a day.

pass the pup

The whole family can join in with this game, which teaches the early stages of recall, and shows your dog that humans are trustworthy. You should all be relaxed and calm for this.

1. Give everyone a handful of treats and sit in a circle, with your dog in the middle.

2. Take turns calling them to you.

3. When they come, feed treats and make a fuss.

Use their name and the command you'll be using, e.g. 'Bella, come!'

did you know?

Licking is a way for a dog to demonstrate they are submissive to someone who is more dominant than they are.

handsome hound

we first groomed our dog on

....

we used

....

....

how they reacted!

....

....

....

welcome home!

the first visitors were

....

....

....

they came on

....

they brought

....

....

....

out and about

Your dog needs to be exposed to as many sights, sounds and smells as possible, so they will feel secure in our human world. This is especially important for young dogs. A shoulder bag or a puppy sling will help if you have a very young puppy or a small breed.

Together we encountered:

- Garden
- Cooking
- TV
- Vacuum cleaner
- Hairdryer
- Ironing board

- Quiet street
- Children
- Men
- Women
- People with hats
- People with sticks

- Busy street with traffic
- Park
- Grass
- Gravel
- A rainy day
- A windy day
- Cars, scooters, lorries, bikes
- Ball games
- Flying kites
- Car park
- Seaside
- Sand
- Countryside
- Mud
- Rivers

- Squirrels, rabbits
- Deer
- Sheep, horses and cows
- Party
- Pub
- A bus ride
- A train station
- A train journey
- Ice
- Snow
- Fireworks
- Daylight
- Dawn
- Dusk
- Darkness

tails from our dog's first outings

they were nervous of

they were excited by

Here is our pooch chilled out at

....

....

....

they were calm and relaxed during

canin e language

Now our pup has lived with us for a few weeks, we can tell
what they're thinking by watching their body language.
This is how we can tell they are:

happy:

over-excited:

scared:

hungry:

just being
greedy!:

bored:

not feeling well:

needing the
toilet:

tired:

over-tired!:

first trip
to the vet

we took our dog to meet the vet on

....

the vet is called

....

they said

....

....

....

Fill in your dog's microchip number and schedule of
vaccinations at the back of the book.

top tip:

Why not take your dog to meet the vet just as a fun outing, so that later visits
– for injections, etc. – won't be scary?

our dog's favourite...

toy

....

spot in the house

....

....

place in the garden

....

....

time of day

....

bath time!

we gave our dog their first bath on

....

because

....

....

....

our dog's thoughts about it!

....

....

....

Before the first bath

After the first bath

tips for
doggy
dental care

Your dog's teeth and gums are as vulnerable to disease as yours so make sure you give their dental health attention and care. Try to do this when your dog is relaxed. (Start doing this early on if you have a puppy so they will get used to it.)

Brushing your dog's teeth daily is the best way to keep your dog's dental hygiene in check.

Some chew bones and chew toys are specially designed to strengthen your dog's gums and teeth.

You should get your dog's teeth checked out by a professional every six to twelve months.

first dental check-up

···

what the vet said

···

···

···

how brushing their teeth went

···

···

···

···

Lots and lots

first play with lead and harness

....

first walk on lead

....

First walk on a lead!

# of fursts!

first walk without pulling

....

first time outside the home off the lead

....

First walk off the lead!

first dry night

....

first sleep through the night

....

first time we heard our dog snoring while they slept

....

first time we saw our dog running in their sleep

....

furst...

sit

lie down

stay

paw

retrieve/fetch

roll over

did you know?

Dogs are scientifically proven to have a calming effect on humans and are often used as part of therapy for people who have been through traumatic experiences – just stroking your pup can lower your blood pressure.

paytime

our dog's favourite games

Playing

ruff and tumble

first play with a new doggy

....

first play date

....

first time told off by an older dog

....

Our dog and friend!

hide and seek

This is a fun obedience-orientated game, which you will need two people for. The great thing about this game is that your dog always gets a win – a huge bonus for dogs that are a little low in confidence.

1. One person gently holds the dog while you run off and hide.

2. Call your dog's name.

3. When you are found, praise your dog and give them treats or a toy.

4. Don't hide too well at first!

barking bad

first time our dog chewed
something they shouldn't

it was

and it belonged to

how to make
DIY dog toys

While shop-bought toys are great, making your own toys can be fun and more cost-effective! Try these ideas and feel free to come up with your own.

Here's my dog playing with their
DIY dog toys!

Sock and Ball

You'll need:

1 sturdy sock

1 old tennis ball

Place the ball inside the sock and tie a knot to seal it inside.

Towel Tug Toy

You'll need:

1 old towel

1. Cut two slits along the length of the towel, equidistant from each other, stopping about 2.5cm from the top.

2. Plait the towel as you would hair.

3. Knot the loose ends.

top tip:

Your dog mustn't start to play until you give the command, e.g. 'Tug!' They must learn to let go when you decide the game is over – for instance, say 'Finished!' and reward them with a high-value treat.

'Everything
I know I
learned
from dogs'

Nora Roberts

oh you
paw thing!

first unwanted guests (fleas, etc.)

....

first roll in something disgusting!

....

it was

....

about the first time our dog was ill

....

....

....

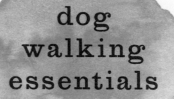

dog walking essentials

Take with you:

- Collar

- Lead

- Harness

- Poo bags (more than one!)

- Dog treats

- Dog!

top tip:

If you have a puppy, walk them for 5 minutes every day for each month of their age, starting when they are around four months old. So at four months you can walk them for 20 minutes. At five months old, 25 minutes, etc.

Winter

● Wellies

● Coat with big pockets

● Jumpers long enough so there
   are no midriff gaps

● Dog coat if your pooch shivers

Summer

A bag for all the essentials:

● Poo bags

● Dog treats

● Drink for you

● Drink for your pup

walkies!

our favourite walk is

....

....

because

....

....

....

....

On our favourite walks

did you know?

Your pup can pick up subtle changes in your scent, which can help them figure out how you are feeling – such as by smelling your perspiration when you become nervous or fearful. It's probably also how dogs can detect certain diseases or know that a household member is pregnant.

doggie paddle

first swim!

....

we were at

....

....

....

First swim!

'A home is never lonely where a loving dog waits'

dog day afternoon

On hot summer days dogs can suffer fatal heatstroke within minutes as they can't sweat. Signs of heatstroke include:

Collapse   Excessive panting   Dribbling

To avoid injury or death in hot weather:

Make sure your dog always has access to water.

Walk at the beginning and end of the day only.

Don't leave your dog in the car – not even with the windows open.

Make ice cubes with your dog's favourite foods – dogs love frozen gravy! Or fill a Kong and put it in the freezer.

Hot pavements can burn your dog's paws. Can you hold the back of your hand on the pavement for five seconds?

If in doubt – have a dog day afternoon inside where it's cool!

make your own pupsicles

Great to help your dog to cool off on hot summer days!

You'll need:

1 banana, peeled

Small pot of plain yogurt

Water

Equipment:

Ice cube trays

Blender

1. Roughly chop the banana and pop into a blender with the yogurt and a splash of water.

2. Whizz until it is a smooth liquid.

3. Pour into ice cube trays and freeze.

The finished pupsicles!

holidogs

our first holiday with our dog was to

....

....

The journey lasted

.... hours

we travelled in

....

....

....

....

how they found the journey

....

....

....

we arrived at our destination

....

we were staying in

....

....

our first trip to the beach when our dog
could run around was at

....

on

....

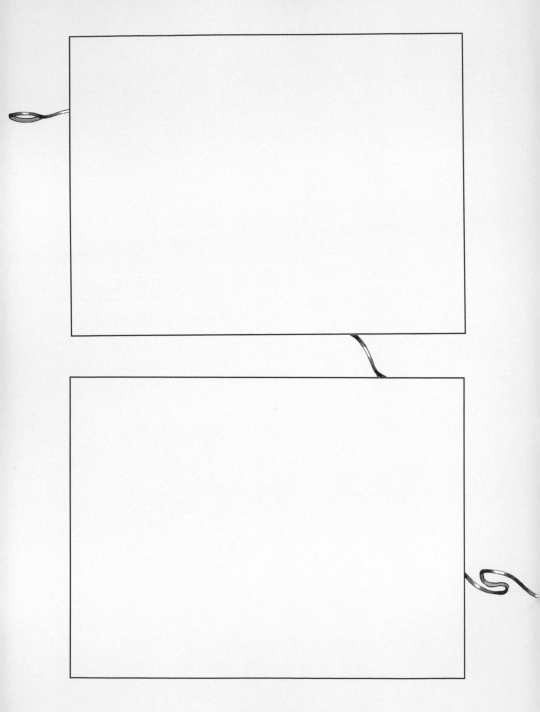

we explored

....

....

....

we played

....

....

....

our dog loved

....

....

....

training classes

we went for classes at

....

our trainer was

....

how it went

....

....

....

....

....

....

At training

gunpowder, whizzes and pops

To keep your dog safe when there are fireworks:

- Make sure they have plenty of exercise during daylight.

- As dusk falls, keep them inside with the curtains drawn.

- Make a cosy den for your dog, making their crate or bed super comfy.

- Turn on the radio or TV to block out the noise of the fireworks.

- Give your dog their favourite toy and a filled Kong, so they have plenty to do.

- If your dog is very nervous during fireworks season, plug-in pheromone sprays (such as Adaptil) and/or anxiety wraps (like Thundershirts) might help. Ask your vet for advice.

how to make your dog a bandana

You'll need:

A nice piece of fabric –
an old shirt or blouse
can work well.

1. Measure your dog's neck and add
   30cm – this gives you .... cm.

2. Now cut a square from the fabric,
   using the measurement above as the
   length of the diagonal of the square.

3. Fold the fabric along the diagonal,
   with the pattern on the inside.

4. Hem 1cm from the two loose edges, leaving just 2cm at one end.

5. Pull the right side of the fabric through the hole, then neatly hand stitch the remaining 2cm.

6. Now knot the bandana around your dog's neck! Always supervise them when they are wearing it to avoid injury.

My pup wearing their bandana!

our pup's
first birthday
with us

their presents were

....

....

....

as a treat we

....

....

....

they ate

....

Birthday fuss!

our favourite memories so far

*very important pup

vip* information

name

vet and phone number

....

....

date of birth

insurance number

....

....

breeder/rescue and
phone number

insurer and
phone number

....

....

injections due

microchip details

....

....

10 9 8 7 6 5 4 3 2 1

Pop Press, an imprint of Ebury Publishing
20 Vauxhall Bridge Road
London SW1V 2SA

Pop Press is part of the Penguin Random
House group of companies whose
addresses can be found at global.
penguinrandomhouse.com

Penguin
Random House
UK

Copyright © Pop Press 2019

Author: Charlotte Cole
Illustrations: Good Wives and Warriors
Design: Emily Voller

First published by Pop Press in 2019

www.penguin.co.uk

A CIP catalogue record for this book is
available from the British Library

ISBN 9781785038617

Printed and bound in China by
Toppan Leefung

MIX
Paper from
responsible sources
FSC® C018179

Penguin Random House is committed to a
sustainable future for our business, our readers
and our planet. This book is made from Forest
Stewardship Council® certified paper.